MUSEUM Shapes

All of the works of art reproduced in this book are from the collections of The Metropolitan Museum of Art.

The Museum's Web site is www.metmuseum.org

Little, Brown & Company

Time Warner Book Group
1271 Avenue of the Americas, New York, NY 10020
Visit our Web site at www.lb-kids.com

First Edition: September 2005

10 9 8 7 6 5 4 3 2 1

Printed in China

Produced by the Department of Special Publications, The Metropolitan Museum of Art:
Robie Rogge, Publishing Manager; Jessica Schulte, Project Editor;
Anna Raff, Designer; Gillian Moran, Production Associate.
All photography by The Metropolitan Museum of Art Photograph Studio, unless otherwise mentioned.

Library of Congress Cataloging-in-Publication Data

Museum shapes / The Metropolitan Museum of Art, NY.—1st ed.
    p. cm.
    "Produced by the Department of Special Publications, The Metropolitan
Museum of Art"—ECIP t.p. verso.
    ISBN 0-316-05698-7 (Little, Brown and Company)
    ISBN 1-58839-134-5 (The Metropolitan Museum of Art)
    1. Shapes—Juvenile literature. I. Metropolitan Museum of Art (New York, N.Y.)
QA445.5.M87 2005
516'.15—dc22

2004026615

MUSEUM Shapes

WITHDRAWN

THE METROPOLITAN MUSEUM OF ART • New York

LITTLE, BROWN AND COMPANY

New York ⋅ Boston

What shape decorates
            the harlequin's costume?

SQUARE

What shape is the wheel?

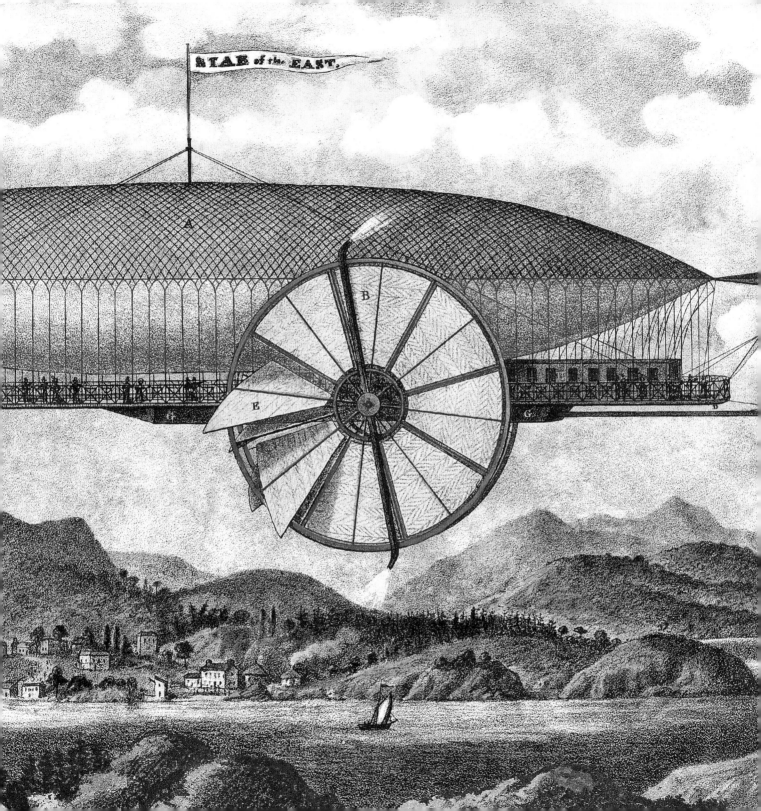

CIRCLE

What shape are the flags?

RECTANGLE

What shape is the man's hat?

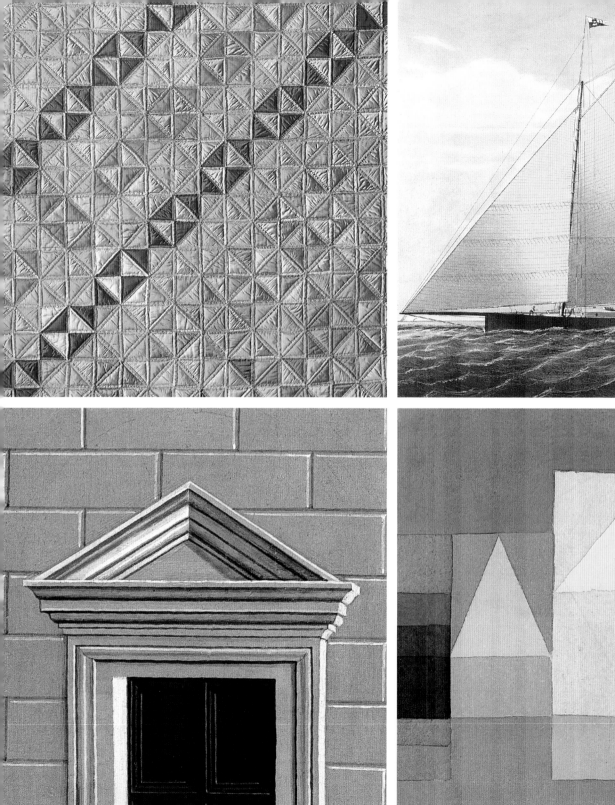

TRIANGLE

What shape is
the woman's hand mirror?

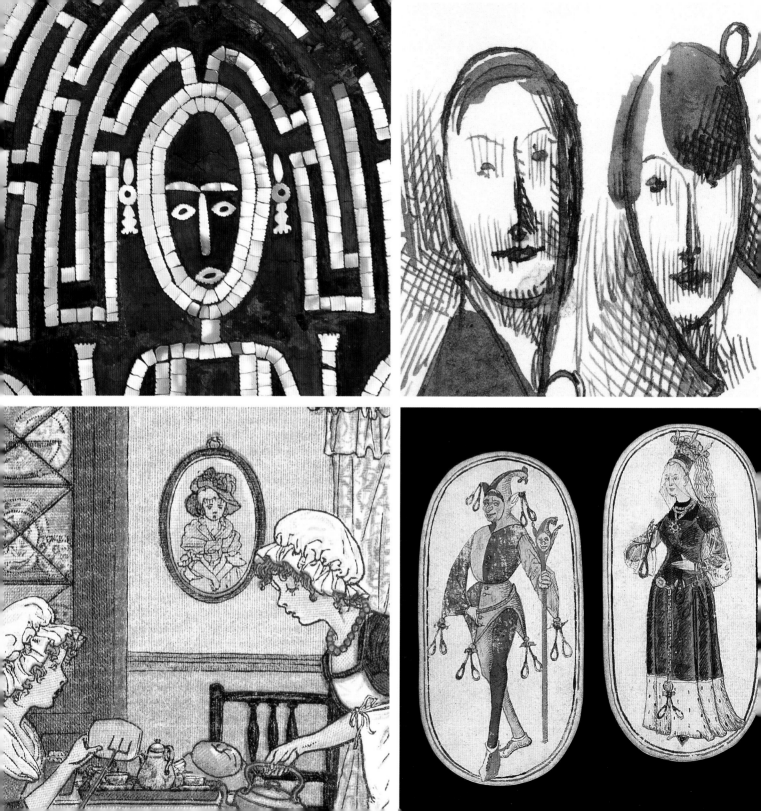

OVAL

What shape is
the opening in the cliff?

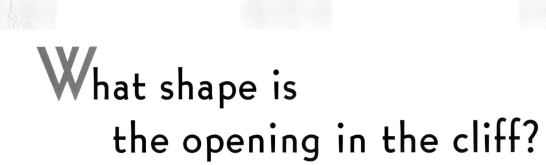

ARCH

What shape is the moon?

CRESCENT

What shape is on the baby's jumper?

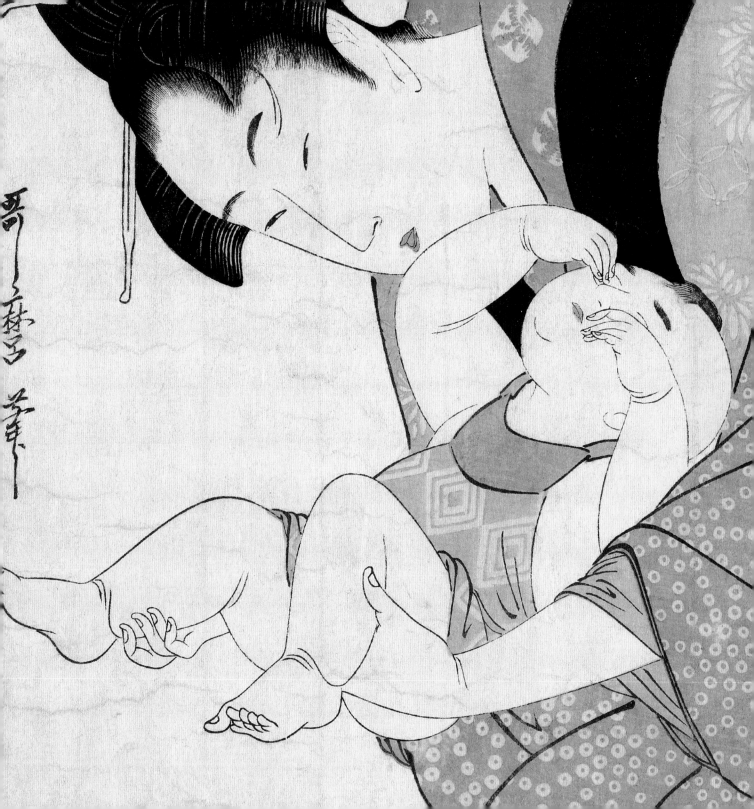

DIAMOND

What shape is the man's book?

HEART

What shape is the angel holding?

STAR

The captions correspond to the pictures at the top of each column, reading clockwise from top left.

Harlequin (detail)
Pablo Picasso, Spanish, 1881–1973
Oil on canvas, 32⅞ x 24¼ in., 1901
Gift of Mr. and Mrs. John L. Loeb, 1960   60.87

Kirtlington Park Dining Room, Set for Tea (detail)
Susan Alice Dashwood, British, active 1886–1900
Watercolor on paper, 13¼ x 19¼ in.
Edward Pearce Casey Fund, 1993   1993.28

Homage to the Square: Young
Josef Albers, American (b. Germany), 1888–1976
Oil on Masonite, 23¾ x 23½ in., 1951–52
George A. Hearn Fund, 1953   53.174.1

Bustan (Garden of Perfume) by Sa'di:
Malik-i-Salih, the King of Syria, Conversing
with Two Dervishes (detail)
Uzbekistan (Bukhara), Safavid period,
ca. mid-16th century
Ink, colors, and gold on paper, 11½ x 7¾ in.
Frederick C. Hewitt Fund, 1911   11.134.2
Folio 80v

Chess and Goose Game Board
Northern Italian or Indian, 17th century
Side 1: chess; ebony, ivory, gold wire, green-
dyed bone, red-brown-dyed horn on a hard-
wood, probably cherry or teak, core, 17 x 16½ in.
Pfeiffer Fund, 1962   62.14

Prince's, Aerial Ship. Star of the East! (detail)
Norris Lithography Firm, American,
mid-19th century
Hand-colored lithograph, 8 x 12⅞ in.
Gift of Paul Bird Jr., 1962   62.696.16

Pawbha: Mandala of Chandra,
God of the Moon (detail)
Indian (Nepali), late 14th or early 15th century
Paint on cloth, 16 x 14¼ in.
Gift of Mr. and Mrs. Uzi Zucker, 1981   1981.465

Cooper in Fujimihara Field in Owari
Province (detail)
Katsushika Hokusai, Japanese, 1760–1849
From the series *Thirty-six Views of Mount Fuji*;
color woodblock print, 10 x 15 in., 1823–29
The Howard Mansfield Collection, Purchase,
Rogers Fund, 1936   JP 2557

The Creation of the World and the Expulsion of
Adam and Eve from Paradise (detail)
Giovanni di Paolo, Italian (Sienese), active by
1417, d. 1482
Predella panel from an altarpiece; tempera and
gold on wood, 18¼ x 20½ in., 1445
Robert Lehman Collection, 1975   1975.1.31

Presentation Quilt (detail)
Probably Mary Simon, American, 1810–?
Cotton and silk velvet; 8 ft. 10¼ x 8 ft. 7¾ in.,
ca. 1849
Sansbury-Mills Fund, 1974   1974.24

Avenue of the Allies, Great Britain, 1918 (detail)
Childe Hassam, American, 1859–1935
Oil on canvas, 36 x 28⅞ in., 1918
Bequest of Miss Adelaide Milton de Groot
(1876–1967), 1967   67.187.127

The Lute Player (detail)
Jane Freilicher, American, b. 1924
Oil on canvas, 36 x 36 in., 1993
Kathryn E. Hurd Fund, 1995   1995.133

Procession Carrying Rekhmira's Equipment to
His Tomb (detail)
Egyptian, Thebes, Sheikh abd el Qurna, 18th
Dynasty
Copy of a wall painting from the tomb of
Rekhmira, 1 ft. 10⅞ in. x 9 ft. 11¾ in., ca. 1475 B.C.
Egyptian Expedition of The Metropolitan
Museum of Art, Rogers Fund, 1930   30.4.80

Townscape: Wall of a Bedroom from the Villa of
P. Fannius Synistor at Boscoreale (detail)
Roman, Second Style, ca. 40–30 B.C.
Fresco on lime plaster, room: H. 8 ft. 8½ in. x W.
10 ft. 11½ in. x L. 19 ft. 7⅛ in.
Rogers Fund, 1903   03.14.13

The Artist's Letter Rack (detail)
William Michael Harnett, American, 1848–1892
Oil on canvas, 30 x 25 in., 1879
Morris K. Jesup Fund, 1966   66.13

Portrait of a Surgeon (detail)
Netherlandish, 1569
Oil on wood, 8¼ x 6¼ in.
Theodore M. Davis Collection, Bequest of
Theodore M. Davis, 1915   30.95.287

Broken Dishes Quilt (detail)
American, ca. 1920
Silk and cotton, 77 x 76½ in.
Sansbury-Mills Fund, 1973   1973.205

Cutter Yacht "Scud" of Philadelphia (detail)
Nathaniel Currier, American, 1813–1888, after
J. E. Butterworth
Color lithograph, 16¼ x 23½ in., 1855
Gift of Adele S. Colgate, 1951   51.567.14

Three Houses (detail)
Paul Klee, German, 1879–1940
Watercolor on paper, bordered with watercolor,
7⅞ x 11⅞ in., 1922
The Berggruen Klee Collection, 1984
1984.315.30

Three Miracles of Saint Zenobius (detail)
Botticelli, Italian (Florentine), 1444/45–1510
Tempera on wood, 26½ x 59¼ in.
John Stewart Kennedy Fund, 1911   11.98

Lady Lilith (detail)
Dante Gabriel Rossetti, British, 1828–1882
Watercolor on paper, 20 x 16⅝ in., 1867
Rogers Fund, 1908   08.162.1

Shield (detail)
Solomon Islands, 19th century
Basketry, mother-of-pearl, paint, H. 33¼ in.
The Michael C. Rockefeller Memorial
Collection, Gift of Nelson A. Rockefeller, 1972
1978.412.730

Dancing Couple (detail)
Elie Nadelman, American, 1882–1946
Pen and ink, and wash on paper, 9¾ x 8 in.,
1917–18
Gift of Lincoln Kirstein, 1965   65.12.11

*Queen and Knave from Suit of
Game Nooses*
Netherlandish, ca. 1470–80
Pasteboard with pen and ink, tempera and
applied gold and silver,
each approximately 5¼ x 2¼ in.
The Cloisters Collection, 1983   1983.515.41–.42

*Illustration from "Mother Goose, or The Old
Nursery Rhymes"* (detail)
Kate Greenaway, British, 1846–1901
Woodcut, printed in color, 6¾ x 5⁵⁄₁₆ in., 1881
Rogers Fund, transferred from the Library,
1921   21.36.98

The Manneporte (Étretat) (detail)
Claude Monet, French, 1840–1926
Oil on canvas, 25⅝ x 32 in., 1883
Bequest of William Church Osborn, 1951   51.30.5

*London: Saint Paul's and Old London
Bridge* (detail)
Antonio Joli, Italian (Venetian), b. about 1700,
d. 1777
Oil on canvas, 42 x 47 in.
Bequest of Alice Bradford Woolsey, 1970
1970.212.2

Railway Bridge at Nogent-Sur-Marne (detail)
Jean-Baptiste-Armand Guillaumin, French,
1841–1927
Oil on canvas, 23¼ x 28⅞ in., 1871
Robert Lehman Collection, 1975   1975.1.180

A Corridor in the Asylum (detail)
Vincent van Gogh, Dutch, 1853–1890
Black chalk and gouache on pink Ingres paper;
24¼ x 18½ in., 1889
Bequest of Abby Aldrich Rockefeller, 1948
48.190.2

Inside Kameido Tenjin Shrine (detail)
Utagawa Hiroshige, Japanese, 1797–1858
From the series *One Hundred Famous Views of
Edo*; color woodblock print, 14⅛ x 9⅜ in., 1858
The Howard Mansfield Collection, Purchase,
Rogers Fund, 1936   JP 2517

Cypresses (detail)
Vincent van Gogh, Dutch, 1853–1890
Oil on canvas, 36¾ x 29⅛ in., 1889
Rogers Fund, 1949 49.30

The Tiburtine Sybil Shows Augustus the Virgin and Child (detail)
Pol, Jean, and Herman de Limbourg, French, active ca. 1400–1416
From *The Belles Heures of Jean, Duc de Berry*
Ink, tempera, and gold leaf on vellum, 9⅜ x 6 11/16 in., 1406–08
The Cloisters Collection, 1954 54.1.1 folio 26v

Plate F II from Astronomicum Caesareum (detail)
Petrus Apianus, German (Ingolstadt), ca. 1490–1559
Hand-colored woodcut, 17⅝ x 12 3/16 in., 1540
Gift of Herbert N. Straus, 1925 25.17

Portions of a Costume Armor (detail)
Attributed to Kolman Helmschmid, German, 1470–1532
Steel and gold, ca. 1525
Gift of Bashford Dean, 1924 24.179
Mrs. Stephen V. Harkness Fund, 1926
26.188.1–.2

The Drowning of Britomartis (detail)
From the series *Scenes from the Story of Diana*
Probably designed by Jean Cousin the Elder, French, ca. 1490–1560
Probably workshop of Pierre II Blasse, French (Parisian), ca. 1547–59
Wool and silk, 15 ft. 3 in. x 9 ft. 7 in.
Gift of the children of Mrs. Harry Payne Whitney, 1942 42.57.1

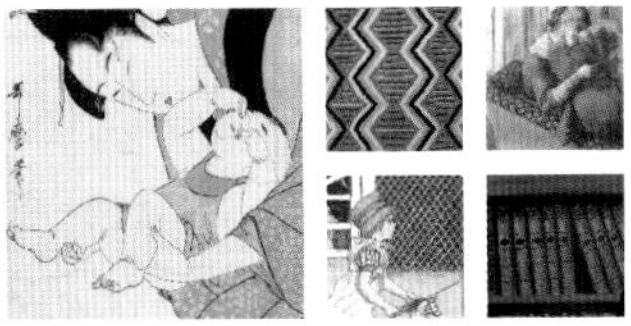

Mother and Sleepy Child (detail)
Kitagawa Utamaro, Japanese, 1753–1806
Color woodblock print, 14⅜ x 9⅝ in., ca. 1795
Rogers Fund, 1922 JP 1278

Wearing Blanket (detail)
Navajo peoples, American (Arizona), 1860–70
Wool, 69 x 48 in.
The Michael C. Rockefeller Memorial Collection, Bequest of Nelson A. Rockefeller, 1979 1979.206.1039

At the Milliner's (detail)
Edgar Degas, French, 1834–1917
Pastel on five pieces of wove paper, backed with paper and laid down on canvas, 27¼ x 27¼ in., 1881
The Walter H. and Leonore Annenberg Collection, Gift of Walter H. and Leonore Annenberg, 1997, Bequest of Walter H. Annenberg, 2002 1997.391.1

Elijah Boardman (detail)
Ralph Earl, American, 1751–1801
Oil on canvas, 83 x 51 in., 1789
Bequest of Susan W. Tyler, 1979 1979.395

Illustration from "Mother Goose, or The Old Nursery Rhymes" (detail)
Kate Greenaway, British, 1846–1901
Woodcut, printed in color, 6¾ x 5 5/16 in., 1881
Rogers Fund, transferred from the Library, 1921 21.36.98

Young Man Holding a Book (detail)
Master of the View of Sainte Gudule, Netherlandish, ca. 1480
Oil on wood, 8¼ x 5⅛ in.
Bequest of Mary Stillman Harkness, 1950
50.145.27

Love Token with Heart and Flower Motifs in Fractur and Cut Work (detail)
American, ca. 1800
Watercolor on white paper, Diam. 13 in.
Gift of Mrs. Robert W. de Forest, 1933
34.100.65

Page from an Illustrated Manuscript (detail)
German, after 1561
Tournament book; pen and colored wash on paper, 13⅝ x 9⅞ in.
Rogers Fund, 1922 22.229

Valentine
American, ca. 19th century
Color lithograph, cut and layered, 4⅝ x 4½ in.
Jefferson R. Burdick Collection, Gift of Jefferson R. Burdick, 1947
Album 606 p. 3v(3)

Letters (detail)
Priscilla Roberts, American, 1916–2001
Oil on canvas, 30¼ x 25 in., 1956–57
Purchase, Elihu Root Jr., Gift, 1957 57.87

Postcard (detail)
Franz Karl Delavilla, Austrian, 1884–1967
Color lithograph, 5½ x 3½ in., 1908
Museum Accession, 1943   WW#19

Woman and Child Catching Fireflies (detail)
Eshōsai Chōki, Japanese, ca. 1785–1805
Woodblock print; ink and color on mica ground,
14¹¹⁄₁₆ x 9⅞ in., ca. 1793
H. O. Havemeyer Collection, Bequest of Mrs.
H. O. Havemeyer, 1929   JP 1739

Plate (detail)
English (Staffordshire), ca. 1825–40
Earthenware, Diam. 8½ in.
Gift of Mrs. Robert W. de Forest, 1933
34.100.93

The American Star (George Washington) (detail)
Frederick Kemmelmeyer, American, ca.
1775–1821
Oil and gold leaf on paper, 22 x 17¾ in., ca. 1803
Gift of Edgar William and Bernice Chrysler
Garbisch, 1962   62.256.7

*Double Frontispiece from a Qur'an
Manuscript* (detail)
North African, 18th century
Ink, color, and gold on paper, 7³¹⁄₃₂ x 5¹¹⁄₃₂ in.
Purchase, Gift of George Blumenthal, by
exchange, 1982   1982.120.2

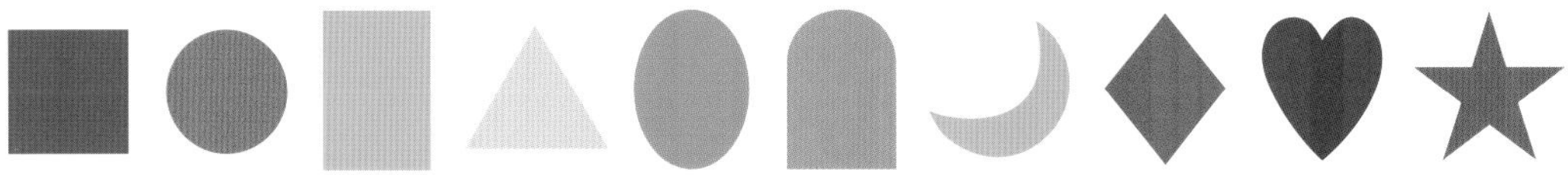